LONDON

THE CITY AT A GLANCE

30 St Mary Axe
The unusual profile of this additio[n]
City has led to its nickname – the
See p012

Tower 42
Despite being rebranded, reclad and tarted up,
most Londoners still know Richard Seifert's
1980 monolith as the NatWest Tower.
25 Old Broad Street, EC2

Tower Bridge
Possibly the most photographed building in
London, Horace Jones and John Wolfe Barry's
engineering marvel was completed in 1894.

City Hall
Lord Foster's 2002 City Hall was built to house
new layers of civic administrative machinery.
The Queen's Walk, SE1

Bank of England
Nikolaus Pevsner called Herbert Baker's
1925-1939 near-obliteration of Sir John Soane's
building a 'great architectural crime'.
Threadneedle Street, EC2

Shakespeare's Globe
The brainchild of the American actor Sam
Wanamaker, the Globe is a 1997 recreation
of a theatre demolished in 1644.
21 New Globe Walk, SE1

Tate Modern
This vast modern art museum is housed in
Sir Giles Gilbert Scott's former power station.
See p010

St Paul's Cathedral
This once unmissable London icon is slowly
being dwarfed by neighbouring developments.
St Paul's Churchyard, EC4

INTRODUCTION
THE CHANGING FACE OF THE URBAN SCENE

For all its luxurious fixtures and fittings, London is not always an easy city to enjoy. It is tough and sprawling and inscrutable, violently fluid and fickle. It is full of cliques and protected spaces, of neighbourhoods entirely at odds with each other. If the Great Recession has dampened the city's good-times vibe, it hasn't dampened it much. Regeneration is still happening apace. But just as the focal point of the city seems to shift eastwards (a pull accelerated by the preparations for the 2012 Olympics), the most staid and traditional areas suddenly burst back into life. See Mayfair – the born-again buzz of Berkeley Square and arrival of Mount Street and Dover Street as new fashion crawls.

Twenty years ago, London's claim to be one of the world's greatest cities was unconvincing. Now it is perhaps *the* global city. And then there are the people. Every talented son or daughter of Europe and beyond, or so it seems, tries their luck in London, seeing if they can make it fly. Many of them are manning the incredible restaurants, bars, cafés and stores that London throws at you. From establishment-cool Notting Hill to emerging-cool Hackney, you are as likely to hear Spanish, French or Slavic spoken as English.

The problem is plotting a course through it all, as London scatters its treasures far and wide. We can think of no other city in the world that requires so much insider nous to navigate properly. And that is where we come in, of course.

ESSENTIAL INFO
FACTS, FIGURES AND USEFUL ADDRESSES

TOURIST OFFICE
Britain and London Visitor Centre
1 Lower Regent Street, SW1
T 0870 156 6366
www.visitlondon.com

TRANSPORT
Car hire
Avis
T 0844 581 0147
Hertz
T 0870 846 0002
Transport for London
T 7222 5600
www.tfl.gov.uk
Taxis
London Black Cabs
T 0795 769 6673
Radio Taxi
T 7272 0272

EMERGENCY SERVICES
Emergencies
999
Police (non-emergencies)
27 Savile Row, W1
T 7437 1212
24-hour pharmacy
Zafash
233-235 Old Brompton Road, SW5
T 7373 2798

EMBASSY
US Embassy
24 Grosvenor Square, W1
T 7499 9000

MONEY
American Express
156a Southampton Row, WC1
T 0870 600 1060
www.travel.americanexpress.com

POSTAL SERVICES
Post office
1 Broadway, SW1
T 0845 722 3344
Shipping
UPS
T 0845 787 7877
www.ups.com

BOOKS
Brick Lane by Monica Ali (Black Swan)
London Architecture
by Marianne Butler (Metro Publications)
London: The Biography
by Peter Ackroyd (Anchor)
The London Blue Plaque Guide
by Nick Rennison (Sutton)

WEBSITES
Art
www.ica.org.uk
www.tate.org.uk
Design
www.designmuseum.org
www.100percentdesign.co.uk
News/Newspapers
www.bbc.co.uk/london
www.guardian.co.uk
www.timesonline.co.uk

COST OF LIVING
Taxi from Heathrow Airport to city centre
£55
Cappuccino
£2.50
Packet of cigarettes
£6.20
Daily newspaper
£0.90
Bottle of champagne
£70

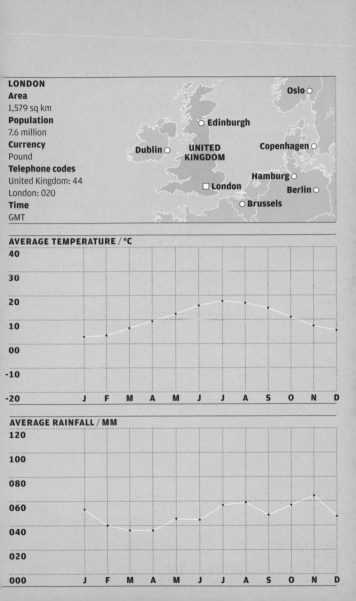

LONDON

Area
1,579 sq km

Population
7.6 million

Currency
Pound

Telephone codes
United Kingdom: 44
London: 020

Time
GMT

Oslo

Edinburgh

Dublin UNITED
KINGDOM

Copenhagen

Hamburg

Berlin

London

Brussels

AVERAGE TEMPERATURE / °C

40											
30											
20											
10											
00											
-10											
-20	J	F	M	A	M	J	J	A	S	O	N	D

AVERAGE RAINFALL / MM

120											
100											
080											
060											
040											
020											
000	J	F	M	A	M	J	J	A	S	O	N	D

NEIGHBOURHOODS
THE AREAS YOU NEED TO KNOW AND WHY

To help you navigate the city, we've chosen the most interesting districts (see below and the map inside the back cover) and colour-coded our featured venues, according to their location; those venues that are outside these areas are not coloured.

CENTRAL

London's West End is really the centre of the modern city. Bloomsbury, spiritual home of the literati, is a kind of oasis, as is Marylebone, now a foodie and interiors destination. Soho has lost some steam to Shoreditch as a nocturnal playground, while Mayfair is where you'll find the grandest hotels, including Claridge's (see p024).

NORTH

Traditionally, the hills of north London have had a more bohemian air than the west. Primrose Hill is among the city's most desirable enclaves, Camden gets crammed with tourists, while King's Cross is undergoing an ambitious urban overhaul, with St Pancras as its focal point.

THE CITY

This is the world's most important business district by some way; the huge wages of the 'City boys' spill west into first-rank clubs and restaurants. The area is a mix of glittering towers, cranes and Victorian pubs, largely deserted come night-time, although the lack of residents is now attracting hip clubs.

WEST

Notting Hill can seem like a fantasy of London, with white stucco townhouses, the chicest boutiques and eateries, and London's most picturesque street market, Portobello. The sheer pleasantness of it all can unnerve some, though visitors may believe they have found an urban idyll.

WESTMINSTER

This is the administrative centre of Britain, site of royal palaces and once the seat of an empire the likes of which the world had never seen. It is the country's antique and wheezing engine room. Our tip is to visit Tate Britain (Millbank, SW1, T 7887 8888), then take the river boat to the South Bank for the grandest of views.

EAST

This area has been transformed and has dragged the epicentre of London cool sharply eastwards. Clerkenwell, especially near Smithfield Market, is where designers, architects and commercial creatives live, work and eat, at venues such as St John (26 St John Street, EC1, T 7251 0848).

SOUTH-EAST

The opening of Tate Modern (see p010) in 2000 forced Londoners to accept that the South Bank was worth a look. The Design Museum (Shad Thames, SE1, T 7403 6933), here since 1989, has been significant in regenerating the area, while Borough Market (see p070) is a big draw for foodies.

SOUTH-WEST

This area is purest posh, with some of the most expensive property on the planet. You can't move for lords, ladies, oil-funded Arab royalty, Russian oligarchs and the odd Hollywood A-lister. It is also where you will find some of London's finest restaurants, such as Olivomare (see p054).

LANDMARKS
THE SHAPE OF THE CITY SKYLINE

It's hard to imagine now, but 50 years ago a portrait of the London skyline was a celebration of the smaller, gentler things in life. Quaintness was the city's stock-in-trade. Until the early 1960s, the height of new buildings was prescribed, not by some cunning and far-reaching architectural masterplan, but by how high a fireman's ladder could reach – about 30m, as it happened. Inevitably, it all changed later in the decade. The BT Tower (see p014), looking like a *2001: A Space Odyssey* film set *avant la lettre* and built to harness the then fabulously exotic microwave technology, seemed like a manifestation of an altogether better future.

Today, that function is fulfilled in The City by Foster + Partners' 30 St Mary Axe (see p012). A similarly massive and iconic presence, as with the BT Tower it seems to be the final destination at the end of every major street, like one of the large buddhas in Bangkok, a startling if benign tumour. Trellick Tower (see p015) is just as obvious a reference point in west London, if less universally revered (JG Ballard allegedly based his novel *High-Rise*, in which tenants begin floor-on-floor warfare, on this tower block). Ernö Goldfinger's landmark, too, has become a cult item, featured in pop songs and on T-shirts. And Trellick Tower has become highly desirable property, the defining icon of modernism's rehabilitation and of the city's acceptance of its radically changing face.

For full addresses, see Resources.

Tate Modern

When the Swiss architects Herzog & de Meuron created a sister gallery to Tate Britain (T 7887 8888), in a former power station in south-east London, it seemed like madness. Today, it's a poster child for the regenerative power of architecture. However, the rawness of Sir Giles Gilbert Scott's original building remains the real point. Work has started on a Herzog & de Meuron designed extension.

Bankside, SE1, T 7887 8888, tate.org.uk

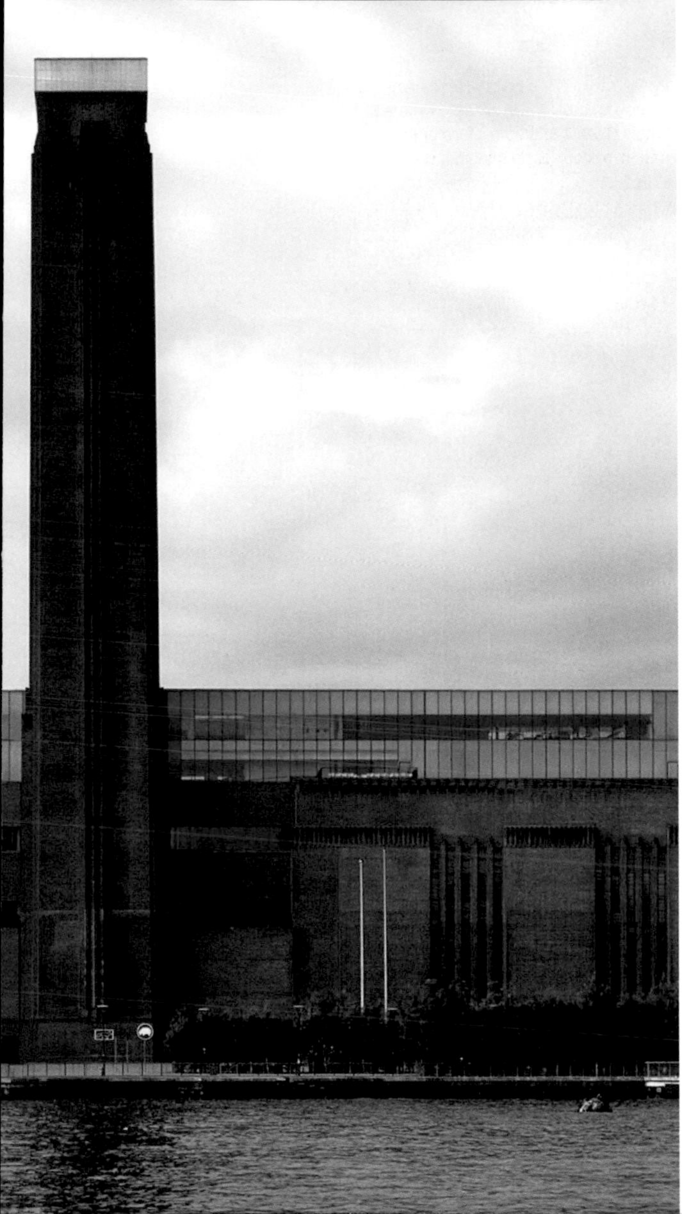

30 St Mary Axe

Completed in 2003, Foster + Partners' 'Gherkin' or, more properly, 30 St Mary Axe, dominates the City skyline. Actually designed by Lord Foster's former chief lieutenant, Ken Shuttleworth (the man behind Hong Kong's Chek Lap Kok airport), the Gherkin swells at its mid-point and tapers to a glass dome, which houses one of the world's most desirable staff canteens, part of which has been re-opened as a members bar. Its cigar shape means that the public spaces at the base are not blighted by the street-level hurricanes that traditional towers produce. Inside, it is divided into a series of coiling atriums and gardens, opening up the space and linking the 40 floors – far more than a series of stacked shelves for worker ants.

30 St Mary Axe, EC3, 30stmaryaxe.com

Centre Point

Richard Seifert's influence on the London cityscape is unmatched (cast an eye over his 1962 creation Space House at 45-49 Kingsway, WC2), but not always in a good way. When this office development opened in 1966, it was the tallest building in London. It was also, famously, one of the most underutilised. The developer, Harry Hyams, wanted to rent the whole building to a single tenant and, as a result, it stood empty for many years. Schemes to turn it into housing have been mooted over the decades, but it seems that its legacy will be as a pointer to shoppers on Oxford Street, and to the power of the property developer's greed. A members' bar, Paramount, on the top three floors, designed by Tom Dixon, has become one of the city's most dramatic nightspots.
101 New Oxford Street, WC1

BT Tower

Unusually for an instantly recognisable landmark, during the first 30 years of its existence, the BT Tower did not appear on any maps. As a microwave relay station for the national phone company, it was an unlikely beneficiary of the Official Secrets Act, and surely the only one with a revolving restaurant on top. But then, ever since it was jointly opened in 1966 by a noted left-wing politician and the owner of a chain of holiday camps, the tower has always been a mix of contradictions. The restaurant closed following a terrorist bomb in 1971 and telecoms technology overtook it soon after, but it is still in operational use and the restaurant is now occasionally open for corporate events.
60 Cleveland Street, W1

Trellick Tower

Ernö Goldfinger's tower block looms over the stuccoed townhouses and chichi eateries of Ladbroke Grove, a last blast of quality brutalism in the UK. Goldfinger started work on the 31-storey tower in 1968 and it was completed in 1972. The look of Trellick Tower is of a monumental concrete slab with add-ons, and is defined by the separate service tower, connected to the 'living units' in the main building by concealed walkways every third floor, with a cantilevered boiler house hanging above it. The apartments themselves are huge, for social housing, with large windows and balconies. And Goldfinger took obsessive care of the details. The balconies have cedar cladding, while the windows are double-glazed and spin round for ease of cleaning.
5 Golborne Road, W10

HOTELS

WHERE TO STAY AND WHICH ROOMS TO BOOK

In Claridge's (see p024), The Dorchester (Park Lane, W1, T 7629 8888), The Savoy (Strand, WC2, T 7836 4343) and The Ritz (150 Piccadilly, W1, T 7493 8181), London has a collection of the most famous hotels in the world – landlocked Titanics, all massive deco ballrooms and gilded doormen. It also claims two Starck/Schrager collaborations, The Sanderson (50 Berners Street, W1, T 7300 1400) and St Martins Lane (see p031); as well as The Lanesborough (Hyde Park Corner, SW1, T 7259 5599), the Lexus of the luxury hotel world; various tiny, appealing townhouse operations (see p026); and in Kit and Tim Kemp's Firmdale empire, an ambitious and uniquely British boutique operation (see p027). There are also quality one-off establishments, such as One Aldwych (see p030) and The Zetter (86-88 Clerkenwell Road, EC1, T 7324 4444).

In east London you can find Terence Conran's The Boundary (see p028), as well as Shoreditch House's (Ebor Street, E1, T 7739 5040) recent Shoreditch Rooms, while more edgily East is the new Townhall Hotel & Apartments (Patriot Square, E2, T 7871 0460). Back in Soho is the cosy Dean Street Townhouse (69-71 Dean Street, W1, T 7434 1775). Meanwhile, Mayfair's *grandes dames* have had facelifts. Look to The Connaught (see p041), the Four Seasons (Hamilton Place, W1, T 7499 0888) and The Savoy, which after major overhauls should emerge phoenix-like late in 2010.

For full addresses and room rates, see Resources.

40 Winks

If we are going to recommend a two-room hotel with a shared bathroom on the Mile End Road, then there has to be something going on. And at 40 Winks, there is, and a lot of it. The four-floor Queen Anne townhouse is owned by interior stylist David Carter whose design approach while less restrained than we usually like, does display a sure touch with over-stuffed set pieces. The hotel is squarely aimed at media types who are more concerned with visual stimulation than round-the-clock service. The hotel is establishing itself as a venue for chichi happenings, like the Bedtime Story evenings. For a charge, guests can hear national treasure actors – Julie Christie and Helena Bonham-Carter – read short stories in person. *109 Mile End Road, E1, T 7790 0259, www.40winks.org*

Double Bedroom, 40 Winks

The Berkeley

This hotel is a conglomeration of high-chic eateries with very well-appointed but rather staid rooms up top. The tiny Blue Bar, designed by David Collins, has queues most nights, while Marcus Wareing at The Berkeley (T 7235 1200), also by Collins, is a theatrical home for one of the city's finest restaurants and darling chefs. The Caramel Room offers a fashion-themed Prêt-à-Portea afternoon tea and the poshest cakes in town. If that isn't enough, The Berkeley has a rooftop pool with a retractable roof and views across London, and one of the best spas in town. One of our favourite accommodations is the Berkeley Suite (above).
Wilton Place, SW1, T 7235 6000,
www.the-berkeley.com

B+B Belgravia

There aren't that many bed-and-breakfast operations with Ingo Maurer chandeliers in the hallway, but the Belgravia is a major step up from the traditional B&B in the design and service stakes. The 17 rooms aren't enormous, but they are blessedly free of chintz – Room 7 (above) is our top choice – and all the bathrooms were renovated in 2009. The smartly modern communal lounge offers free internet access, tea and coffee, and an open fire. There is no restaurant or bar, but breakfast is served overlooking a lovely garden, and there's also a free bike borrowing service. A few words of warning: there's no lift, and don't expect liveried footmen. But for a smart Georgian townhouse in London's toniest quarter, it's a steal.
64-66 Ebury Street, SW1, T 7259 8570, www.bb-belgravia.com

Claridge's

This might be the de facto HQ of the European aristocracy, but not even a hotel of Claridge's standing can afford to rest on its laurels. All of London's great hotels have had to update to survive, and none has done so as successfully as this. The public rooms, including Gordon Ramsay's eponymous restaurant (T 7499 0099) – one of the best in town – have been restored to breathtaking effect by New York architect Thierry Despont. Ramsay is Britain's most notorious cook, and the Chef's Table gives you the option of eating while the famously short-tempered Scot and his staff do their business around you. And, we love this, the elevator has its own driver and sofa. The best room is the Brook Penthouse (left), restored to its 1930s finery. It has a private roof terrace and its own butler. *Brook Street, W1, T 7629 8860, www.claridges.co.uk*

Dukes Hotel

This posh pad is famous for three things: unapologetically rococo Brit furnishings; an almost spookily peaceful location overlooking Green Park; and perhaps the best martinis in town, mixed by Gilberto in Dukes Bar. All of this is reason enough to check in. But in 2007, Dukes was bought by Campbell Gray Hotels, the owners of One Aldwych (see p030), who have undertaken a complete renovation, while keeping the plump country-house styling. Dukes is now on its way to establishing itself in the very top tier of London hotels. Not that it's a fusty proposition as it stands. All the rooms have wi-fi and plasma TVs, there's a 24-hour gym and a rather marvellous little art collection. Ask for one of the Junior Suites (above). *St James's Place, SW1, T 7491 4840, www.dukeshotel.com*

Haymarket Hotel

The sixth hotel in the Firmdale empire, the Haymarket builds on the formula that has proved so winning at the Covent Garden (T 7806 1000), Charlotte Street (T 7806 2000) and Soho (T 7559 3000) outposts. The 50 rooms and suites are all unique and decorated in the group's trademark amped-up, off-kilter, English-country-house style, like Room 3 (above). The colour scheme runs through turquoise and fuchsia, which Kit Kemp pulls off, while the public rooms are all elegant oak. What really sets the place apart, though, is its host building, designed by John Nash, the starchitect of Regency London, and an 18m pool with a sound and light system, pewter bar and capacity for a throng of 300.
1 Suffolk Place, SW1, T 7470 4000, www.firmdale.com

The Boundary

Opened in January 2009, this hotel tickles almost all our fancies. It's small, only 12 rooms and five suites; there's a great restaurant, The Boundary; a rooftop garden and grill; and a café/deli combo, The Albion. Each of the rooms has a theme, so, among others, there is a Bauhaus room (pictured), and Eileen Gray room. *2-4 Boundary Street, E2, T 7729 1051, www.theboundary.co.uk*

One Aldwych
Perhaps the best of the wave of London hotels to have opened in the noughties, One Aldwych was created by architects Jestico + Whiles in a wonderful flatiron Edwardian building, once home to *The Morning Post*. The lobby (above) is a white, double-height, art deco-cum-futuristic fantasy, and while the rooms and corridors are perhaps a little 'W', the hotel's collection of contemporary art helps lift them out of bog-standard deluxe. There are two fine restaurants, Axis and Indigo, and the 18m basement pool, with piped underwater music, is a treat. The location is great too – it's a short walk to the Thames and Covent Garden.
1 Aldwych, WC2, T 7300 1000,
www.onealdwych.com

St Martins Lane

Opened in 1999, seven months before The Sanderson (see p016), and immediately eclipsed by it, St Martins Lane is the less expensive but more likeable and better located of Ian Schrager's two Starck-designed London hotels. Housed in a 1960s office block, the design motifs are similar: Kubrick sci-fi and antique French fancies. The oversized gnomes and gold molars in the lobby can quickly bore, but there is still a restraint here, as in The Light Bar (above), which is lacking in some of Starck's other efforts. The floor-to-ceiling windows in the 204 rooms allow fantastic views of the city. And mood lighting allows guests to turn their all-white space various vivid colours, so at night St Martins Lane becomes a fantastic sort of Rothko canvas. *45 St Martin's Lane, WC2, T 7300 5500, www.stmartinslane.com*

24 HOURS

SEE THE BEST OF THE CITY IN JUST ONE DAY

London's parks are its saving grace. Without them the city would be unliveable, huge and unremitting. They are, perhaps, the prize for living in a city of massive sprawl with an overstretched public transport system. The more manicured and planned Royal Parks of central London can seem like bizarre indulgences, while the larger, 'wilder' Hampstead Heath in the north and Richmond Park in the south are like countryside-replacement patches for the struggling urbanite. But these parks are not denials of the city; they are an intrinsic part of it, where locals spend time, run and court.

Our day starts with a hearty breakfast at Automat (opposite) in the heart of the revitalised Mayfair, before a short post-waffle waddle across the road for retail therapy at Comme's multi-floor, multi-brand emporia, Dover Street Market (overleaf). Lunch is at the always-humming Cecconi's (see p036), yet more evidence that Nick Jones, the man behind Soho House (40 Greek Street, W1, T 7734 5188) and Shoreditch House (see p040), can do no wrong. Then we head to Hampstead Heath (see p037), a landscaped slice of Arcadian fantasy, of shades and glades, pools and ponds. Close the day with the sort of high-quality 'pub grub' that is the city's greatest culinary innovation of the last decade. There were plenty of options but we decided to head over to the handsome Georgian terraces of Barnsbury and the Drapers Arms (see p038).

For full addresses, see Resources.

09.00 Automat

It is hard not to see updates of the classic American diner as somewhat cynical route-one restaurateuring. But Mayfair's 'American brasserie' is too fashionable a breakfast spot to ignore. And at least it is run by a New Yorker – an adopted one anyway – the Argentine-born architect-turned-restaurateur Carlos Almada. The interior is pure stage set: a wood-and-leather 1950s railway carriage leading to a larger, white-tiled room. The breakfast menu, available from 7am, includes Bourbon-vanilla French toast with streaky bacon, and brunch is served from 11am at weekends. Almada has opened a bar, club, restaurant and library beneath Automat, which is quite the celebrity haunt. He plans to add a swimming pool beneath that.
33 Dover Street, W1, T 7499 3033, www.automat-london.com

10.30 Dover Street Market

Mindful that the super-architect-designed 'luxury box' was becoming a cliché, Comme des Garçons' Rei Kawakubo opened DSM in a tired Georgian townhouse-turned-office in 2004, spending a piffling £800,000 on the refurb, gutting the place and giving it a cursory paint job. Interior design, such as it is, was left to film and set designers. Essentially, Kawakubo's guerrilla store concept is a collection of 'shabbily' artful stalls put together by designers such as Givenchy, Lanvin, Dior Homme, her own various Comme incarnations and some more esoteric set-ups, such as retro-hardware store, Labour & Wait (see p074), and vintage gown dealer, Decades. DSM can also be credited with leading the retail migration west of Bond Street.
17-18 Dover Street, W1, T 7518 0680, www.doverstreetmarket.com

13.30 Cecconi's

This restaurant was opened in a prime Mayfair spot in 1978 by Enzo Cecconi, the youngest ever general manager at the Cipriani in Venice. It introduced London to Italian fine dining and to bellinis and beef carpaccio. It also pioneered the idea of provocative pricing, charging £8 for half a watermelon. But despite or because of this, it established itself as one of the capital's most fashionable eateries. Hard times hit and the restaurant closed in 1999. It was taken over by Nick Jones of Soho House in 2005 and given a decorative going-over by Ilse Crawford. Now an airy space of aquatic green and glass, it is once again a haunt of the smart set. Jones has becalmed the menu to offer classic fare. Try the *cichetti*, the Italian version of tapas. *5a Burlington Gardens, W1, T 7434 1500, www.cecconis.co.uk*

16.30 Hampstead Heath

Hampstead Heath is 3.2 sq km of wetland, woodland, meadows and urban ramblers, just over 6km from central London. For many Londoners, it is hard to imagine surviving the city without regular trips to the Heath and its ersatz rusticity. Among its hot spots are: Parliament Hill, which affords probably the best views of London there are; Kenwood House (T 8348 1286), with its library designed by Robert Adam (the venue for popular outdoor classical concerts on summer evenings); and the bathing ponds, one mixed and two gender-specific. Hampstead Heath is also emblematic of an ideal of north London as a hilly, pleasant place, where liberal people live with their dogs and large book collections. In truth, the whiff of bohemia dissipates year by year. *NW3, www.cityoflondon.gov.uk*

20.00 Drapers Arms

Islington's Drapers Arms is reliably at or near the top of London's gastro pub league table. The establishment is run by Nick Gibson and Ben Maschler, the son of Britain's most feared restaurant critic, while the kitchen is led by St John alumnus Karl Goward. Formal dining is available upstairs and something less high falutin' at the ground-floor bar.
44 Barnsbury Street, N1, T 7619 0348

URBAN LIFE
CAFÉS, RESTAURANTS, BARS AND NIGHTCLUBS

London has a nightlife proposition to rival any city. Its dining scene matches New York's for its vibrancy, and, at the top end at least, the city boasts some of the world's finest restaurants. The irascible Scot, Gordon Ramsay, is now trying his hand at gastro pubs. Meanwhile the far more likeable Mark Hix – a godfather of new British cooking, as influential as Fergus Henderson of St. John restaurant (see p060) – grows his own empire, HIX (see p050).

Dean Street Townhouse (see p061), yet another Nick Jones project, marks a sort of revival for Soho, long over-taken by Shoreditch as London's Boho quarter. Jones hasn't given up on the new East though, opening Pizza East (see p049) in the Tea Building, the now landmark building topped off by his Shoreditch House (Ebor Street, E1, T 7739 5040). The tapas and sort-of-tapas trend gathers pace with Dehesa (see p057) and Polpo (see p045).

The gastropub is now established at the heart of the London dining scene with The White Swan (see p048), Anchor & Hope (36 The Cut, SE1, T 7928 9898) and the Bull & Last (168 Highgate Road, T 7267 8955), just three of the stars. London's bar life throws up the possibility of any kind of night out, from glitzy to downtown funky, with the East challenging the West as a nightlife draw. While, the hipsters are heading north-east following a migratory pattern along Columbia Road, up Broadway Market and on to Dalston. *For full addresses, see Resources.*

Connaught Bar

Built in 1897, The Connaught is the very definition of the London luxury hotel as urban country house. It has promised and delivered discretion and a fierce resistance to novelty. By 2004 though, when it was bought by the Maybourne Hotel Group (owners of Claridges and the Berkeley), the Connaught was considered a little too Woodhousian to be entirely healthy. The ensuing £70m overhaul has included the complete reimagining of its two bars. India Mahdavi redesigned the Coburg Bar, while heavyweight champ of bar designers David Collins has added oodles of glamour to the Connaught Bar (which has its own entrance on Mount Street). The interior cocoons you amid marble and black leather banquettes and silver leaf walls. *Carlos Place, W1, T 7499 7070, www.the-connaught.co.uk*

Lounge Bohemia
Opened in late 2007, the only clue
to alert you to the existence of Lounge
Bohemia is a narrow stairway decorated
with Czech newspapers. Downstairs,
it's all mid-century furnishings and
glassware by Czech designer Jiri Pelcl.
Czech-inspired canapés are served
on Riki Watanabe trays.
1E Great Eastern Street, EC2,
T 077 2070 7000

Albion

Part of Sir Terance Conran's Boundary Hotel, the Albion Café, or Caff, as they prefer is dedicated to superior treatments of British comfort food. Festival of Britain modernism and fish and chips is not a new tactic – see Canteen, which has seriously fizzled of late – but the Albion does it exceedingly well. The interior – all white tiles, warm minimalism and painted tin – is expertly arranged and the egg and bacon butties, steak and kidney pud, and bread and butter pudding are prepared with the right amount of care and innovation. A lot of the former, not too much of the latter. The Albion also includes a shop piled neat and high with British product and produce, and an excellent bakery that tweets when its buns and such are fresh out of the oven. *2-4 Boundary Street, E2, T 7729 1051, www.albioncaff.co.uk*

Polpo

Polpo is the kind of bar/restaurant they do effortlessly in Nolita or the Lower East Side – bare bricks, baroque tin ceiling, small square tables and no dinner reservations – but that seems laboured whenever someone makes a stab at similar in London. Polpo has pulled the trick off so successfully that it is just about the most fashionable joint in town. The concept is relocated *bacaro* – a particular sort of Venetian bar dealing in Italianate tapas. Polpo has installed itself in the basement of an 18th century Soho house that was once home to Canaletto. And while every second restaurant that opens in the capital right now seems to offer tapas, Polpo is up there with Dehesa (see p057) in terms of quality.
41 Beak Street, W1, T 7734 4479,
www.polpo.co.uk

Bob Bob Ricard
Another Collins' designed restaurant
and with a plumb corner spot on Soho's
Golden Square – Bob Bob Ricard is
a high-end riff on between-the-wars
railway chic; leather booths and
tarnished brass fittings. The menu
is mostly posh comfort food served
from breakfast to dinner, 7am to 3am,
which may be a record in London.
1 Upper James Street, W1, T 3145 1000

White Swan

In 2003, from what was once the Mucky Duck, emerged the White Swan on Fetter Lane near Fleet Street. It was one of the first of a family of excellent gastro pubs run by Tom and Ed Martin that now includes The Botanist in Sloane Square, The Hat and Tun on Hatton Wall, The Cadogan Arms on the King's Road in Chelsea, The Well in Clerkenwell and the Prince Arthur in London Fields, famed for its deep fried jam sandwich dessert. The brothers opened the White Swan before they had fully embraced the modish new-Victoriana interiors that mark out their later openings. And, unlike other pubs, it boasts a separate, more contemporary dining room on a different floor to the real ale and bar snacks. *108 Fetter Lane, EC4, T 7242 9696, www.thewhiteswanlondon.com*

Pizza East

Nick Jones, the man behind the Soho House group, is not infallible. The lifts at Shoreditch House are small and break down, and frankly the members' list should be seriously rethought. But when he gets things right, which is most of the time, he gets them very right. Jones' new Pizza East, based he says on LA's Pizzeria Mozza and housed on the ground floor of the Shoreditch's now landmark Tea Building (with Shoreditch House perched on top), is one of a new wave of high quality pizza joints in the capital. The Clam and veal balls, amongst other options, come on small but pillowy bases. There is a good selection of antipasti. The large interior space features exposed piping and concrete, stretches of leather, and a deli. *56 Shoreditch High Street, E1, T 7729 1888, www.pizzaeast.com*

HIX

Former Japanese restaurant Aaya has
become HIX, the third of Mark Hix's
establishments. As chef director of
Caprice Holdings, Hix has championed
British food, which is why the menu does
marvellous things with black pudding
and mash, and includes entrées like
'Manx queenies with wild boar bacon'.
66-70 Brewer Street, W1, T 7292 3518,
www.hixsoho.co.uk

Corrigan's Mayfair

The most fashionable chef of the moment, Richard Corrigan, serves up large dollops of rustic, seasonal fare with a heavy emphasis on game at a new, eponymous restaurant in Mayfair. Where else? The flavoursome food hits the sweet spot of contemporary tastes, while the interior is by Martin Brudnizki, the designer of Scott's and the Ivy Club.
28 Upper Grosvenor Street, T 7499 9943

Olivomare

Mauro Sanna opened Olivo (T 7730 2505) in 1990, pushing a sophisticated take on the food of his native Sardinia. He followed that with the less formal Oliveto (T 7730 0074) in 1995, serving some of the best pizza in London. Sanna then upped the ante again in 2007, opening Olivomare, an upscale seafood restaurant, and Olivino, an adjoining shop/deli. Sanna now has a mini and much-loved empire in London's poshest postcode. As with its predecessors, Olivomare was designed by Sardinian architect Pierluigi Piu. It's entirely white, with one wall given over to a laminate geometric repeat fish print. The food is almost universally good. Try some sea urchin and baby octopus, or simpler options like chargrilled monkfish.
10 Lower Belgrave Street, SW1,
T 7730 9022, www.olivorestaurants.com

L'Anima

Architect Claudio Silvestrin has pulled off the expensive minimalist aesthetic at L'Anima, engineering a space of cool drama with travertine floors and marble bathrooms. The bar and kitchen areas are separated from the main dining room by glass walls, while the porphyry walls of the bar area are the perfect complement to the white leather sofas. A curving corridor leads to a walk-in wine-tasting room and an extraordinary private dining room with a green marble table. The chef and co-owner is Francesco Mazzei, formerly of St Alban, who cooks up excellent, mostly southern Italian, food. Try the *zitoni*, *n'duja* and aubergine (tube-shaped pasta with spicy salami), followed by dark-chocolate iced truffle. *1 Snowden Street, EC2, T 7422 7000, www.lanima.co.uk*

Scott's

This restaurant has had the likes of Oscar Wilde and Ian Fleming through its doors over the past 150 years. By the end of the last century, though, Scott's had become the preserve of ageing pinstripes. It was acquired by Caprice Holdings in 2005 and designer Martin Brudnizki was called in to bring back the glam – and he's worked a treat. Scott's is updated deco done with real panache, marked as utterly contemporary with artworks by Gary Hume and Fiona Rae, among others, and a giant crustacean shelf from Future Systems. There are oak and marble mosaic floors and an onyx-topped, stingray-skinned oyster bar. With head chef Kevin Gratton producing some of the best seafood in town, the dining experience is complete. *20 Mount Street, W1, T 7495 7309, www.scotts-restaurant.com*

Dehesa

Most assume that brunch is a Californian or Antipodean meddling in the natural order or things: posh fry-up for idlers, festering in bed disguised as an aspirational lifestyle option. In fact, the British invented brunch, name and concept, back in 1895, though we still view the idea with some suspicion. Dehesa, a tapas bar/charcuterie and sister to the excellent Salt Yard, is, amongst other things, doing its utmost to make brunch an elevated sort of weekend indulgence rather than a quick hangover fix. Toasted sourdough with scrambled duck egg, and roasted foie gras with fried eggs and patatas fritas are highlights. They do also do a hell of a Bloody Mary though, with a follow-on of churros and hot chocolate for good measure.
25 Ganton Street, W1, T 7494 4170, www.dehesa.co.uk

The Loft Project
Portuguese post molecularist Nuno
Mendes is now doing his tricksy thing
at Viajante at Townhall Hotel (see p016)
in Bethnal Green. He has a turned his
Loft Project private dining club over to
a rotating roster of young international
chefs of similar intent. Join just 15 other
guests at a communal table for superb
10-course tasting menus.
T 7956 205 005, www.theloftproject.co.uk

St John Bread & Wine

Fergus Henderson, a trained architect, cooks with a sort of modernist clarity of purpose. And his Clerkenwell restaurant, St John (T 7251 0848), certainly has a white-walled, spare seriousness about it, while his modern British menu, with its famous emphasis on offal, is puritan in its lack of elaboration. With St John firmly established among the Clerkenwell creative set since 1994, Henderson branched out in 2003 with St John Bread & Wine in Spitalfields. As the name suggests, this space is part bakery, part wine shop, as well as an all-day restaurant, with a simpler menu than the mother ship. Breakfast is especially good; order the smoked Gloucester Old Spot bacon sandwich.
94-96 Commercial Street, E1, T 7251 0848, www.stjohnbreadandwine.com

Dean Street Townhouse

Between the late 1920s and late 1970s, 69-70 Dean Street in Soho was home to David Tennant's Gargoyle Club. The aristocratic nighthawk wanted his club to be a place where the well-born could get close to the demi monde. Eventually the club got closer to the demi monde than was probably wise. The conjoined townhouses now have a new and happier life as a 39-bedroom hotel (see p016) and all day-

dining room, run by Soho House's Nick Jones. You could argue that what Jones has done here is entirely predictable, at least on the restaurant front. It's a clubbable Brit brasserie with an English revival menu and 60-piece collection of contemporary Brit art. Predictable indeed, but it is so well executed that resistance is futile. *69-71 Dean Street, W1, T 7434 1775, www.deanstreettownhouse.com*

INSIDER'S GUIDE

NATASHA GILBERT, MODEL

Natasha Gilbert is a model, presenter for MTV and reporter for fashion website handbag.com. Well travelled but a Notting Hill resident, Gilbert likes to start her day with an egg. Or two. 'The best eggs are at <u>Raoul's</u> (105-107 Talbot Road, W11, T 7229 2400),' she insists. For coffee, Gilbert heads to the organic café, <u>The Tea and Coffee Plant</u> (180 Portobello Road, W11, T 7221 8137). Lunch is often in the West End at the Great Marlborough Street branch of Henry Dimbleby's conscience-saving good fast food chain, <u>Leon</u> (35 Great Marlborough St, W1, T 7437 5280).

Evenings out frequently mean a trip to Will Ricker's Notting Hill establishment <u>E&O</u> (14 Blenheim Crescent, W11, T 7229 5454) for 'inventive cocktails' and Asian food, or to <u>Firezza</u> (12 All Saints Road, W11, T 7221 0020) for fantastic (take away or eat-in) pizza. 'For live music I like to grab a drink at <u>Ronnie Scott's</u> (47 Frith Street, W1, T 7439 0747) and listen to some jazz,' she says. One of the world's great jazz clubs, the venue had a multi-million pound makeover in 2006. For a livelier night out, Gilbert heads East to the Cat & Mutton (76 Broadway Market, E8, T 7254 5599) on Broadway Market, home to a furiously busy food and vintage clothing market on Saturdays. Alternatively, she loves the <u>Dalston Superstore</u> (117 Kingsland Road, E8, T 7254 2273), a raw-chic diner by day that turns into a super-charged club after 10.00pm.

For full addresses, see Resources.

ARCHITOUR
A GUIDE TO LONDON'S ICONIC BUILDINGS

When Ernö Goldfinger's cinema at the Elephant & Castle in south London was torn down in 1988, it was little lamented. In those days, London seemed to be determined only to replace its modernist heritage with anodyne office blocks peddling nothing more interesting than 1980s aspiration. That the city largely failed in that mission is one of Europe's better kept architectural secrets. London's modernist legacy is one of its least appreciated treats.

Nowhere, save the better stations on the Jubilee Line extension, such as Canary Wharf and Southwark, can remove you so totally from the blitzed, burned and otherwise edited mess of histories that make up the city as the Barbican development does. Walk along its elevated walkways and lakes set in concrete and you are in a cohesive retro futurescape, a fragment of a different city. On a single night at the end of 1940, 142,000 sq m of an area north of the City was destroyed by bombs. Though the first plans for the wasteland's redevelopment were drawn up by Chamberlin, Powell & Bon in 1955, their work was not completed until the opening of the Barbican Centre arts complex (overleaf) in 1982. By then, it looked out of date. Today, it looks like a dream. We've picked that project and three other modernist gems, and thrown in the expert extention of the Whitechapel Gallery (see p069), to make up a gentle half-day's architourism.
For full addresses, see Resources.

Economist Building

Peter and Alison Smithson were (almost) the Charles and Ray Eames of postwar Britain; among the country's most important modernists and creators of the 'new brutalist' movement. In truth, they talked and theorized more than they built but The Economist Building – actually three Portland stone towers set around a plaza in swishy St James and completed in 1964 – is their masterpiece. Their clients had insisted that they build a hymn to modernity, with 'no fake antiquarianism'. And that is certainly what they delivered.
25 St James's Street, SW1

Barbican

Architects Chamberlin, Powell & Bon had complete control of the Barbican development, right down to the doorknobs. Finally, it would include three towers of more than 40 storeys each, seven terrace blocks, one seven-storey tower, a church, two schools and the Barbican Centre arts complex (in truth, something of an afterthought). The architects referenced Frank Lloyd Wright and Le Corbusier, but created something unique, working on it from 1955 until 1982. The concert hall has recently been improved by Caruso St John and Alford Hall Monaghan Morris. And where the Barbican was once a little lost in a forgotten part of town, it is now in the heart of the fashionable 'east side', which seems absolutely right.
EC2, T 7638 4141, www.barbican.org.uk

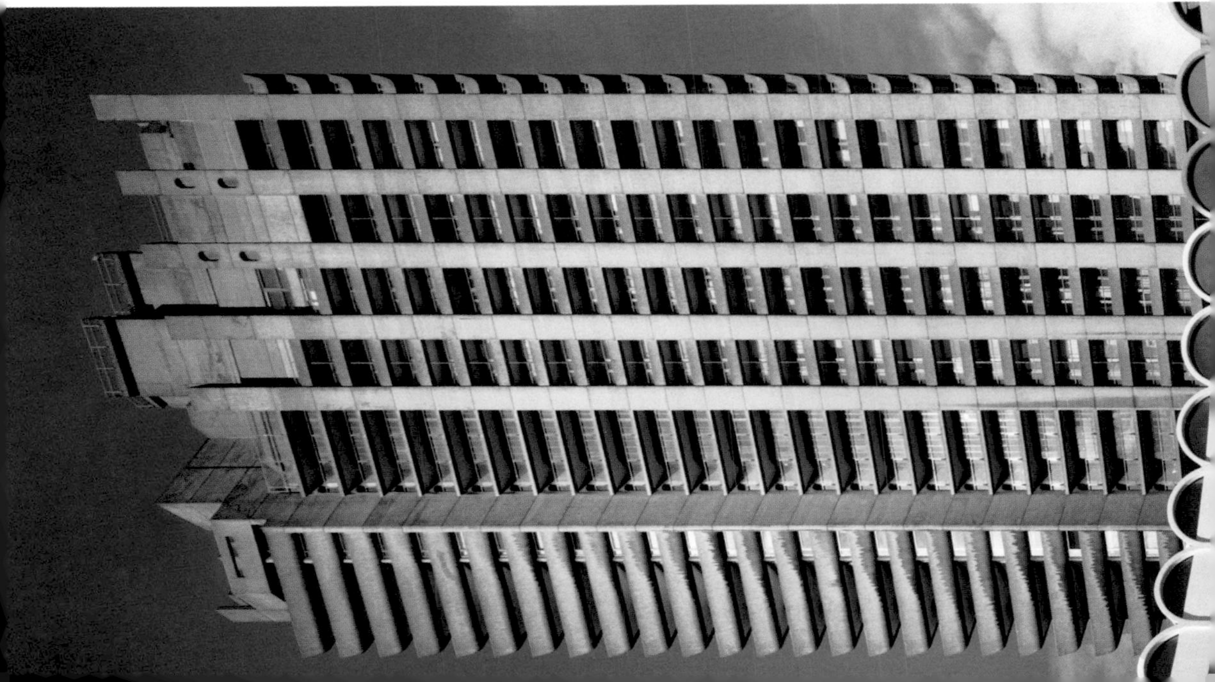

National Theatre

This is the most visible and controversial piece of concrete architecture in London, the loudest example of heroic modernism in the capital. Denys Lasdun's scheme had to include three theatres and all sorts of backstage apparatus and spaces, as well as cafés, bars and foyers. To a degree, all this pressure on the space shows. Yet the building remains one of the most dramatic to grace the River Thames – the perfect expression of Lasdun's ambition to make landscapes of buildings, tumbling and towering strata, structures that stretch and climb. *South Bank, SE1, T 7452 3400, www.nationaltheatre.org.uk*

Whitechapel Gallery

Opened in East London in 1901, the Whitechapel Gallery was designed to bring art to the area's huddled masses. Since then it has always punched above its weight. It was the first and only British gallery to show Picasso's *Guernica* in 1939 and held the first shows for US artists such as Jackson Pollock and Mark Rothko and for then-emerging British artists David Hockney and Gilbert and George.

Current director Iwona Blazwick has taken over the next door Whitechapel Library in a £13.5m expansion. Designed by Belgium architects Robbrecht en Daem, working with London firm Witherford Watson Mann and the artist Rachel Whiteread, the addition represents an 80 per cent increase in exhibition space (above). *77-82 Whitechapel High Street, E1, T 7522 7888, www.whitechapelgallery.com*

Commonwealth Institute

According to English Heritage, the Commonwealth Institute building is the second most important modern building in London after the Royal Festival Hall. All the more dispiriting then that five years ago it narrowly survived being delisted and dynamited to make way for luxury bunkers for Russian oligarchs. This concrete and brick 'tent', completed in 1962, occupies a plum patch of green off Kensington High Street, next to Holland Park, so you can see the development possibilities. The future now looks considerably rosier for the building as the Design Museum plans to move on and in, though they probably won't have their Minis and Apple Macs in till 2013. Architect John Pawson has been tasked with planning the new museum and reviving the property.
Melbury Court, Kensington High Street, W8

SHOPPING
THE BEST RETAIL THERAPY AND WHAT TO BUY

London has Bond Street, and in Selfridges (400 Oxford Street, W1, T 0800 123 400) and Liberty (see p086), two of the most innovative department stores in the world. But there is a lot more to its retail opportunities than that, from the food and interiors outlets along Marylebone High Street and the surrounding roads, to the sleek boutiques of Lamb's Conduit Street, such as Darkroom (see p082), and the edgier offerings of Shoreditch, including menswear store Present (see p084), which also boasts the best barista in town. Just around the corner Jasper Morrison celebrates super normal design at his diddy and discrete new store (see p076).

And even if Bond Street is entirely predictable, Mayfair, particularly around Bruton Street and Mount Street, has seen some exciting openings, from the Comme des Garçons collective Dover Street Market (see p034) to the Paul Smith Furniture shop (9 Albemarle Street, W1, T 7493 4565).

London has emerged as an art-world hub, with Mayfair and St James's St regaining much of their old lustre from the East End via venues such as White Cube (25-26 Mason's Yard, SW1, T 7930 5373) and Hauser & Wirth (196a Piccadilly, W1, T 7287 2300) with a new larger gallery on Savile Row opening October 2010. Design galleries are also moving in, including the excellent Carpenters Workshop Gallery (3 Albemarle Street, W1, T 3051 5939).

For full addresses, see Resources.

David Gill Galleries
This is one of our favourite resources. David Gill's vast gallery in a disused glove-and-handbag factory in south London is where to go for one-off, modern, sculptural pieces, and works by Barnaby Barford, Fredrikson Stallard, Mattia Bonetti and Zaha Hadid, among others. Items are sold in editions of six to 30, and are the museum collectables of the future. In a separate space within the gallery, Gill sells modern classics by designers such as Charlotte Perriand and Jean Prouvé, such as the 1952 'Tunisie' bookshelf (above, price on request). He also offers art. The original Fulham Road store opened way back in 1987, and Gill has been a key player driving the market for 20th and 21st century design ever since.
3 Loughborough Street, SE11, T 7793 1100, www.davidgillgalleries.com

Labour and Wait
Established in 2000, Labour and Wait
is a celebration of functional design
from an age before anyone thought
to fetishise functionalism. In an artfully
crammed little store, you can pick up
hardware for the kitchen and garden,
as well as clothing and accessories.
Check opening hours before you visit.
18 Cheshire Street, E2. T 7729 6253,
www.labourandwait.co.uk

Jasper Morrison Shop

The British designer Jasper Morrison is having a moment, a very serious moment. After a half decade in which certain elements of the design world got over-excited and over elaborate at being told they were artists and paid accordingly, Morrison held steady with his quietly militant dedication to 'everyday useful objects', the 'supernormal' as he called it. Together with Japanese designer Naoto Fukasawa, Morrison put together an exhibition of the supernormal and this shop, essentially a small unused area of his Shoreditch studio, is a continuation of that project, stocking his own designs as well as those by other designer members of the supernormal crew and anonymous examples of the elegantly functional.
24b Kingsland Road, E2,
www.jaspermorrison.com

Bermondsey 167

The transformation of Bermondsey Street from a downright dangerous stretch of south-east London into a thoroughly civilised shopping destination is one of London's more remarkable examples of chi-chification. Bermondsey 167 was founded by Michael McGrath together with Alessandro Palhares, a designer whose CV includes stints at the good and great of British menswear, including Dunhill, Aquascutum, Gieves & Hawkes and eight years as head of menswear at Burberry. The store carries McGrath's own M2CG collection of menswear, including shirts made in Kent (£98, above) and silk ties (£59) from Italy. The store also sells unique pieces of furniture, homewares and ceramics commissioned by McGrath. *167 Bermondsey Street, SE1, T 7407 3137, www.bermondsey167.com*

Margaret Howell
A long-serving stalwart of British
fashion Margaret Howell has enjoyed
a major renaissance in the last five years
as a champion of clean, immaculately
tailored British casual wear for men
and women. Her flagship store on
Wigmore Street (pictured) is designed
by William Russell of Pentagram.
*34 Wigmore Street W1, T 7009 9006,
www.margarethowell.co.uk*

Albam

What began as an online retail men's clothing operation in Nottingham now has this lovely little unit on Beak Street in Soho, as well as newer stores in Islington and Spitalfields. The label has developed a loyal following doing simple things very, very well. When designing, Albam's founders Alastair Ray and James Shaw seem to ask themselves one basic question: 'Would Steve McQueen wear it?'.

It's the right question to ask and the answer is a tight range of knockabout basics made and cut extremely well. The fisherman's cagoule, tapered chinos and hi-top deck shoes are always in demand. Although most of clothing is produced in the UK the pair do turn, when they need to, to makers in the US, Portugal and Italy. *23 Beak Street, W1F, T 3157 7000, www.albamclothing.com*

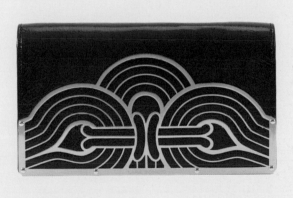

Lara Bohinc

With clients from Madonna to Björk, the beautiful Ms Bohinc might be just about the most fashionable jeweller in the world. Slovenian by birth, she studied industrial design at the Ljubljana Academy of Fine Arts before moving to London to study jewellery design and metalwork at the RCA. She then set up shop in East London's Hoxton Square housing her entire collection of hard-edged yet elegant, architectural accessories. In early 2008 she moved across town to a new shop — designed by Amsterdam and Ljubljana-based architects Elastik — big enough to carry a range that now includes bags and leather accessories. We particularly like her Tatjana Cheque Book Wallet (above, £289).
149F Sloane Terrace, SW1, T 7730 8194, www.larabohinc.com

Darkroom

Thanks to a highly principled landlord, Holborn's Lambs Conduit Street is a focal point of fine independent retailing. One of the newer additions is compact concept store Darkroom. Mixing original high-end fashion and interior accessories, founders and friends Rhonda Drakeford and Lulu Roper-Caldbeck have gone global to source pieces that are both beautiful and unique to the store. The pair are also peddling their own highly covetable designs, as well as hosting bi-monthly art and sculpture exhibitions. Darkroom is worth visiting if for no other reason than to check out the store's immaculate styling. Design duo Matt Edmonds and Pam West of Frank have created bespoke shelving, a cash desk and display cabinets for the shop, while the statement tiled floor was hand-painted by the talented proprietors themselves.

52 Lamb's Conduit Street, WC1, T 7831 7244

Present

For nearly two decades, the Duffer of St
George brand defined a particular strand
of British street style; collegiate casual
wear matched with dashes of updated
English tailoring, part Richie Cunningham,
part Prince Charles. Present is what
Duffer co-founder Eddie Prendergast did
next. The store on Shoreditch High Street
stocks cult US and Japanese brands such
as Gitman Bros, Yuketen and Haversack
as well as a specially produced line of
Trickers brogues – the longtime hipster's
choice of classic British footwear – and
Present's small own label collection.
A particular stroke of genius was installing
world champion barista Gwilym Davies,
and his La Victoria Arduino espresso
machines at the entrance.
140 Shoreditch High Street, E1,
T 7033 0500, www.present-london.com

Mint

Established by Lina Kanafani over a decade ago, Mint is the kind of design store that goes way beyond the usual suspects, commissioning exclusive one-off and limited edition pieces from new and established designers as well as handcrafted glass, ceramics and textiles. The joy of Mint is Kanafani's fearlessness and aversion to the safety of quiet good taste. Mint challenges you to get to grips with Kanafani's selection, to take time and to come back once you have thought it over. It's a strategy that has paid off handsomely, though as of last summer, regular Minters have had to get used to coming back to her new larger store in the Brompton Quarter (above) and not the tiny original on Wigmore Street. *2 North Terrace, SW3, T 7225 2228, www.mintshop.co.uk*

Liberty
Opened on Regent Street in 1875 by Arthur Liberty, dealing in fabrics and exotica, a recent strategic tune up has transformed Liberty into a daring little department store / large concept store. It's fashion departments have the innovative but focused buying skills of a sharp independent rather than exercises in simple label-bagging.
T 7734 1234, www.liberty.co.uk

SPORTS AND SPAS
WORK OUT, CHILL OUT OR JUST WATCH

The 2012 Olympics promise to leave London, specifically Newham in east London, with some fine and architecturally daring sports arenas. But it can already boast what its architect, Lord Foster, calls the finest football stadium in the world in Wembley Stadium (see p094). And we're not going to argue. With its huge illuminated arch, it is one of the capital's iconic structures, and a radical improvement on its predecessor, where facilities, let alone the view of the pitch, were becoming embarrassing, given its international renown.

In truth, fitting sport and fitness into London life does take a little work. But there are sophisticated gyms – try The Third Space (13 Sherwood Street, W1, T 7439 6333) or Matt Roberts' Mayfair gym (16 Berkeley Street, W1, T 7491 9989) – good football pitches (fittingly, Hackney Marshes, the spiritual home of every Sunday footballer, is part of the Olympic zone), excellent climbing centres and a number of fine spas, including the newly upgraded Spa at the Dorchester (see p090) and entirely new Cowshed treatment rooms at Shoreditch House (see p016). One, or rather a number, of London's more neglected treasures are its lidos. Some are being restored, including the lovely London Fields Lido. And, of course, the Thames is famous for its rowing clubs. The provision of cycle lanes in London remains scandalous, but it is getting better, and the number of cyclists on the roads increases exponentially.

For full addresses, see Resources.

Dunhill

In 2008 Dunhill opened a retail store-cum-exclusive members' hangout in an 18th century grand pile – very grand, it was once the home of the Duke of Westminster – just north of Berkeley Square on Davies Street. Our favourite feature of the house is its wonderful spa and barber. The design is a witty and thoroughly welcoming update of the traditional posher sort of gentleman's barber – think Geo F Trumper and the like. So you get your own TV screen to watch a movie while enjoying tonsorial attention. And along with the wet shaves and short, back and sides comes the offer of more modern forms of pampering including sports massages, hot stone massages and facials in its two treatment rooms.

2 Davies Street, W1, T 845 458 0779,
www.dunhill.com

The Dorchester Spa
After a £3.2m upgrade, the spa at the
Dorchester has become an extravagant
art deco-revisited pampering palace;
the design is by Fox Linton Associates.
But the real appeal is the range of
treatments on offer. Facials are by
the very in-demand Vaishaly, with other
treatments by Carol Joy London, Kerstin
Florian and Australian brand Jurlique.
Park Lane, W1, T 7319 7109

Laban

Built in 1998 for a relatively modest £22m, this is still one of the largest and most expensive contemporary-dance centres in the world. It was designed by Swiss architects Herzog & de Meuron and is, many would say, their most important contribution to London's landscape (even if Laban's position on a former rubbish tip in Deptford means not enough people get to see it). Designed in collaboration with artist Michael Craig-Martin, the building is a polycarbonate-coated box that allows views of the shadowy student dancers during the day. At night, it becomes a giant plastic-and-glass lantern, lit up lime, turquoise and magenta. With a 300-seat theatre, Pilates studio, health suite and café and bar, the interior is no less successful. *Creekside, SE8, T 8691 8600, www.laban.org*

Lord's

It's odd that the Marylebone Cricket Club, England's ultra-conservative cricket high court, should commission such an outlandish structure. In fact, the lords of Lord's are quite daring patrons of innovative architecture. Witness Nicholas Grimshaw's grandstand, built around the same time. But it is the Media Centre (above), completed in 1999, that still startles. Designed by architects Future Systems, using shipbuilding and aircraft technology, it was the first all-aluminium semi-monocoque building in the world. And it's not often that we get to say that. The purpose of the centre is to contain all the TV, radio and press people under one roof. Raised 15m above the Compton and Edrich Stands, it looks like the sinister eye of a monstrous machine, which it kind of is. *St John's Road, NW8, T 7616 8500*

Wembley Stadium
Massively over-budget, massively late,
and just plain massive, Foster + Partners'
stadium is a behemoth beached in north-
west London. Designed to seat 90,000
and topped by a 315m single-span arch
(the longest of its kind in the world),
it's an astonishing structure and a grand
symbol of England's sporting obsession.
Empire Way, HA9, T 0844 980 8001,
www.wembleystadium.com

ESCAPES
WHERE TO GO IF YOU WANT TO LEAVE TOWN

London has no Hamptons or Sitges, though the Cotswolds to the west and Norfolk to the north are strong weekend draws, with large populations of Londoners at rest or in exile. Both now have good stocks of delis, design shops, excellent restaurants, old pubs gone gourmet and contemporary country-house hotels, such as Cowley Manor (Cowley, T 01242 870 900) and Babington House (Somerset, T 1373 812 266) that banish the chintz from the English countryside experience. The Olde Bell Inn (see p100) is less grand but just as welcome an innovation, with fabulous country modern interiors.

The Cotswolds has become a serious foodie draw, but it is the village of Bray in Berkshire that has become a genuine international gastro-resort. It is here that the talented Heston Blumenthal cooks up snail porridge, quail jelly and the other iconic dishes of his now notorious 'molecular gastronomy' at the three-Michelin-starred Fat Duck (High Street, T 01628 580 333). Its near neighbour, the similarly starred Waterside Inn (Ferry Road, T 01628 620 691), is run by Michel Roux and his son Alain.

London's nearest major seaside resort is fashionable Brighton, just 80km away. It is full of fine Regency architecture, including the bizarre Royal Pavilion (Old Steine, T 01273 290 900). There are also several fine examples of modernism located close to London, including The Homewood (see p102) in Surrey.

For full addresses, see Resources.

De La Warr Pavilion, Bexhill-on-Sea
Built in 1935, Erich Mendelsohn and
Serge Chermayeff's De La Warr Pavilion,
in Bexhill-on-Sea, was the first modernist
public building in the country. The 1933
competition to build a startlingly modern
seaside entertainment complex was
announced within two months of
Mendelsohn arriving in England, and
the German émigré, already a serious
figure in European architecture, hit the
project at some speed. He created
an impossibly glamorous docked-liner
of a building, with large glass windows
and curving terraces, and an enormous
chrome-and-steel staircase (overleaf).
An £8m restoration by architects John
McAslan has helped to re-establish
the Pavilion as one of the south's most
important cultural buildings.
Marina, T 01424 229 111, www.dlwp.com

The Olde Bell Inn

Opened in 2008, The Olde Bell Inn (10 minutes from Henley-on-Thames) is in some ways simply the boutique-ing and gastro-ising of the traditional British coaching Inn. Rooms that were once fusty and stale-smelling now feature walk-in monsoon showers and Aesop toiletries. But the designer Ilse Crawford has managed to assemble rooms and public spaces that sit comfortably with the history of this wonky Tudor building – indeed some parts date back to 1135. In the dining room, banquettes are brightened with geometric print Welsh blankets, contemporary Thönet bentwood chairs are matched with Matthew Hilton and birch Ercol Windsors, produced in High Wycombe. The food made by chef Tony Abarno – featuring locally sourced ingredients, of course – is excellent.
High Street, Hurley, Berkshire,
T 01628 825 881, www.theoldebell.co.uk

The Homewood, Esher

Esher in Surrey is the heart of the stockbroker belt — wealthy and dull. But it is also the setting of The Homewood, the second modernist property of the National Trust (entry is by booked guided tours only), after Goldfinger's 2 Willow Road (T 7435 6166). The house was designed and built in 1938 by architect Patrick Gwynne for his parents. He was just 24 but already a committed modernist, having worked with Wells Coates and studied the work of Le Corbusier. The house is essentially an open-plan glass-and-air take on the country house, in which Gwynne used marble, terrazzo and gold leaf to stunning effect. He continued with modernism for the rest of his life, but The Homewood remains his finest work. *Portsmouth Road, T 01372 476 424, www.nationaltrust.org.uk*

NOTES
SKETCHES AND MEMOS

RESOURCES

CITY GUIDE DIRECTORY

HOTELS
ADDRESSES AND ROOM RATES

B+B Belgravia 026
Room rates:
double, £125;
Room 7, £125
64-66 Ebury Street, SW1
T 7259 8570
www.bb-belgravia.com

The Berkeley 020
Room rates:
double, from £299;
suite, from £750
Wilton Place, SW1
T 7235 6000
www.the-berkeley.com

The Boundary 028
Room rates:
double, from £140;
suites, from £250;
Bauhaus Room, from £140;
Eileen Gray Room, from £160;
Young British Designers Room,
from £200
2-4 Boundary Street, E2
T 7729 1051
www.theboundary.co.uk

Charlotte Street Hotel 027
Room rates:
double, from £255
15-17 Charlotte Street, W1
T 7806 2000
www.firmdale.com

Claridge's 024
Room rates:
double, from £319;
suite, from £950
Brook Street, W1
T 7629 8860
www.claridges.co.uk

The Connaught 016
Room rates:
double, from £329;
Suite 105/Connaught Suite,
from £3,640
Carlos Place, W1
T 7499 7070
www.the-connaught.co.uk

Covent Garden Hotel 027
Room rates:
double, from £290
10 Monmouth Street, WC2
T 7806 1000
www.firmdale.com

Cowley Manor 096
Room rates:
double, £250
Cowley
Near Cheltenham
T 01242 870 900
www.cowleymanor.com

Dean Street Townhouse 016
Room rates:
double, from £195
69-71 Dean Street, W1
T 7434 1775
www.deanstreettownhouse.com

The Dorchester 016
Room rates:
double, from £655;
suite, from £895
Park Lane, W1
T 7629 8888
www.thedorchester.com

Dukes Hotel 026
Room rates:
double, from £330;
suite, from £595
St James's Place, SW1
T 7491 4840
www.dukeshotel.com

40 Winks 017
Room rates:
double, from £140
109 Mile End Road, E1
T 7790 0259
www.40winks.org

Four Seasons 016
Room rates:
prices on request
Hamilton Place, Park Lane, W1
T 7499 0888
www.fourseasons.com

Haymarket Hotel 027
Room rates:
double, from £250;
Townhouse Suite, from £3,000
1 Suffolk Place, SW1
T 7470 4000
www.firmdale.com

The Lanesborough 016
Room rates:
double, from £495;
suite, from £715
Hyde Park Corner, SW1
T 7259 5599
www.lanesborough.com

The Olde Bell Inn 100
Room rates:
double from, £195
High Street, Hurley
Near Henley-on-Thames
Berkshire, SL6
T 01628 825 881
www.theoldebell.co.uk

One Aldwych 030
Room rates:
double, from £235;
suite, from £495
1 Aldwych, WC2
T 7300 1000
www.onealdwych.com

The Ritz 016
Room rates:
double, from £470
150 Piccadilly, W1
T 7493 8181
www.theritzlondon.com

St Martins Lane 031
Room rates:
double, from £495;
suite, from £1,000
45 St Martin's Lane, WC2
T 7300 5500
www.stmartinslane.com

The Sanderson 016
Room rates:
double, from £545;
suite, from £850
50 Berners Street, W1
T 7300 1400
www.sandersonlondon.com

The Savoy 016
 Room rates:
 prices on request
 Strand, WC2
 T 7836 4343
 www.fairmont.com/savoy
Shoreditch Rooms 016
 Room rates:
 prices on request
 Ebor Street, E1
 T 7739 5040
 www.shoreditchhouse.com
Soho Hotel 027
 Room rates:
 double, from £290;
 suite, from £400
 4 Richmond Mews, W1
 T 7559 3000
 www.firmdale.com
Townhall Hotel & Apartments 016
 Room rates:
 prices on request
 Patriot Square, E2
 T 7871 0460
 www.townhallhotel.com
The Zetter 016
 Room rates:
 double, from £99
 St John's Square
 86-88 Clerkenwell Road, EC1
 T 7324 4444
 www.thezetter.com

WALLPAPER* CITY GUIDES

Editorial Director
Richard Cook

Art Director
Loran Stosskopf

Editors
Rachael Moloney
O'ar Pali

Author
Nick Compton

Deputy Editor
Jeremy Case

Managing Editor
Jessica Diamond

Senior Designer
Eriko Shimazaki

Designers
Dominic Bell
Lara Collins

Map Illustrator
Russell Bell

Intern
Hazel Lubbock

**Wallpaper* Group
Editor-in-Chief**
Tony Chambers

Publishing Director
Gord Ray

Contributors
Sara Henrichs
Meirion Pritchard

Wallpaper* ® is a
registered trademark
of IPC Media Limited

First published 2006
Second edition 2007
Third edition (revised
and updated) 2009
Fourth edition (revised
and updated) 2010
© 2006, 2007, 2009 and
2010 IPC Media Limited

ISBN 978 0 7148 5941 5

PHAIDON

Phaidon Press Limited
Regent's Wharf
All Saints Street
London N1 9PA

Phaidon Press Inc
180 Varick Street
New York, NY 10014

Phaidon® is a registered
trademark of Phaidon
Press Limited

www.phaidon.com

A CIP Catalogue record for
this book is available from
the British Library.

All prices are correct at
time of going to press,
but are subject to change.

Printed in China

PHOTOGRAPHERS

John Arnold Images Ltd/Alamy
Wembley Stadium, pp094-095

Emma Blau
Trellick Tower, p015

Theo Cook
Centre Point, p013
BT Tower, p014
Hampstead Heath, p037
St John Bread & Wine, p060
Scott's, p056

Dennis Gilbert/NTPL
The Homewood, pp102-103

Noemie Goudall
L'Anima, p055

Jason Hawkes/ jasonhawkes.com
London city view, inside front cover

Martin Jordan
Laban, p092

Lee Mawdsley
David Gill Galleries, p073

Chris Parker
De La Warr Pavilion, pp098-099

Simon Phipps
Economist Building, p065

Christoffer Rudquist
30 St Mary Axe, p012
40 Winks, p017, pp018-019
The Berkeley, p020, p021
B+B Belgravia, p022, p023
Dukes Hotel, p026
The Boundary, pp028-029
Dover Street Market, p034, p035
Cecconi's, p036
Drapers Arms, pp038-039
Connaught Bar, p041
Lounge Bohemia, pp042-043
Albion Café, p044
Polpo, p045
Bob Bob Ricard, pp046-047
Pizza East, p049
Hix, pp050-051
Corrigan's Mayfair, pp052-53
Olivomare, p054
Dehesa, p057
The Loft Project, pp058-059
Dean Street Townhouse, p061
Natasha Gilbert, p063
Barbican, pp066-067

Whitechapel Gallery, p069
Commonwealth Institute, pp070-071
Labout and Wait, pp074-075
Jasper Morrison Shop, p076
Bermondsey 167, p077
Margaret Howell, pp078-079
Albam, p080
Lara Bohnic, p081
Darkroom, pp082-083
Present, p084
Mint, p085
Liberty, pp086-087
Dunhill, p089
The Dorchester, pp090-091

Claire Skinner
Lord's, p093

LONDON
A COLOUR-CODED GUIDE TO THE HOT 'HOODS

CENTRAL
The bustling commerce of the West End is leavened by Bloomsbury's cultured calm

NORTH
King's Cross might be arriving but glorious, laid-back Primrose Hill is already there

THE CITY
By day, the increasingly high-rise centre of the financial world; by night, largely deserted

SOUTH-WEST
If you're looking to snare a Russian oligarch or an Arab prince, start your search here

WEST
Stucco central, this is what first-time visitors expect to find everywhere in the city. Sadly

WESTMINSTER
Ditch the coach-party crowds. Get in, get a glimpse of the urban Gothic, then get out

EAST
The focal point of London cool has been shifting here steadily over the past 10 years

SOUTH-EAST
One of the fastest-changing areas of London is heading upwards at a dizzying rate

For a full description of each neighbourhood, see the Introduction.
Featured venues are colour-coded, according to the district in which they are located.